The Junior High Survival Manual

Katrina L. Cassel
Illustrated by Chris Sharp

CPH
SAINT LOUIS

Copyright © 1998 Concordia Publishing House
3558 S. Jefferson Avenue, St. Louis, MO 63118-3968
Manufactured in the United States of America

Library of Congress Cataloging-in-Publication Data

Cassel, Katrina L., 1962–
    The junior high survival manual/Katrina L. Cassel.
      p.   cm.
    Summary: Discusses things a junior high school student needs to know, such as setting goals, keeping good study habits, and improving social skills, and how Christian faith can help in these pursuits.
    ISBN 0-570-05062-6
    1. Junior high schools—United States—Handbooks, manuals, etc.—Juvenile literature. 2. Study skills—United States—Handbooks, manuals, etc.—Juvenile literature. 3. Junior high school students—United States—Conduct of life—Handbooks, manuals, etc.—Juvenile literature. 4. Junior high school students—United States—Religious life—Handbooks, manuals, etc.—Juvenile literature. [1. Study skills. 2. Christian life. 3. Schools.] I. Title.
LB1623.5.C37 1998

1 2 3 4 5 6 7 8 9 10   07 06 05 04 03 02 01 00 99 98

Contents

Introduction

Welcome to junior high! Ahead of you is a whole new world. You are gaining independence, making more decisions for yourself, and confronting more choices about friends, activities, and how you live out your faith.

This book identifies some of the changes you will face in junior high. It addresses skills such as goal setting, time management, and study habits. It also helps you focus on developing positive friendships that will go the distance. This book examines peer pressure, both good and bad, and helps you make your own choices based on God's Word.

Take advantage of the worksheets and try to answer the questions honestly. Doing these activities will help you evaluate what areas you need to work on—goal setting, time management, making friends, or making the right decisions.

Above all, spend time with your heavenly Father, studying His Word. Read about other young people (and adults) who faced challenges—Abraham, Joseph, Samuel, David, Solomon, Naaman's servant girl, Esther, Peter, or Paul. Reflect on how God helped them make tough decisions and how He helped them grow in faith and in love for Him.

God has promised to direct your path. Even when things don't seem to be going well, God is at work to bring about His plans for you. After all, He promised you at your Baptism that He would always be with you—even in junior high!

Katrina Cassel

1

Aim High

Have you ever made resolutions and forgotten them by the next week? Do you want to accomplish things this school year, but don't know how? This chapter will help you set realistic goals and make plans to achieve them.

Jared ran up the school steps with his backpack slung over one shoulder and a gym bag tucked under the other arm.

"How was your summer?" his friend Todd asked.

"Boring as usual. I'm almost glad to be back in school!" Jared answered.

"What? Did I hear you say you're glad to be here?" Todd exclaimed.

"Well, almost. As long as I have to be here, I might as well make this year count," Jared said.

"Now you're talking," Todd said. "What are your plans for this year?"

"Plans?"

"You know, what do you want to accomplish—what are your goals?" Todd asked.

"Goals? I haven't even thought of them. Guess I'm not as organized as you are," Jared said.

"It doesn't take a genius, but I do have a list of goals and a plan for meeting them. That's the best way to accomplish things," Todd said.

The warning bell sounded, interrupting the conversation. Jared and Todd raced for homeroom together.

Your Turn

Someone once said, "*He who aims for nothing always achieves it.*" How about you? If it's true for you, try setting goals and making a game plan to achieve them.

Goals aren't limited to the beginning of a new school year or New Year's Day—start today!

*Choose areas
for improvement*

Stop and think about your study skills, school performance, and daily life. What needs improvement? Do old habits need breaking, or does a new habit need to be formed? Are there hobbies you want to learn or talents/skills you want to improve? Do you want to make more friends or better grades? Think about the following areas. Which do you want to improve or change?

- Musical talent
- Sports and fitness
- Spiritual growth
- Academic progress
- Relationships
- Artistic or creative ability

*Choose one or
two focus areas*

Limiting your choices allows you to give more time and thought to specific areas for improvement. You may decide to improve your academic performance and your fitness level or to achieve more in your Christian walk and relationships. Decide which areas are most important to you. You can always change your mind or add new choices later as you meet your goals.

Many people make New Year's resolutions but fail to keep them. Most resolutions are too vague and lack focus. "I will exercise" or "I will read my Bible every day" are good resolutions, but go a step farther to set a more specific goal.

- *Be decisive about your targeted areas.* You are more likely to be successful in achieving goals in the areas that interest you or concern you most.

- *Decide exactly what it is you want to accomplish.* Go beyond a general statement, such as "improving my grades," to a more specific area, such as "improving my test scores in history class" or "improving my gym grade by cutting my time on the obstacle course."

- *Know your end point.* What will you have accomplished when your goal is complete? Do you want to make As on every history test during the first grading period? Or do you want to achieve passing test grades all year? What time do you need to achieve on the obstacle course to improve your overall gym grade? Know your end point and you will have a clearer idea of how to achieve it.

*Talk to God
about your goals*

God knows you better and loves you far more than any human can. After all, He sent His only Son to win your salvation on the cross. He knows what you can accomplish. He knows the plans He has for you. Ask Him for wisdom in setting and achieving goals.

As you read or listen to God's Word, pay attention to those passages that apply to your goals. For example, James 1:5 says: "If any of you lacks wisdom, he should ask God, who gives generously to all without finding fault, and it will be given to him." Or if you want to know God's view about being prepared, read Matthew 25:1–13. How do passages like these relate to your earthly goals? your spiritual goals?

Finally, trust in God's promise to give you the strength to follow through. Philippians 4:13 says, "I can do everything through [Christ] who gives me strength." God will help you accomplish a goal that He wants for you.

Make a
game plan

Now that you have a list of specific goals, you need a plan to accomplish them. The plan gives you a step-by-step map to completion.

1. *Ask yourself, "What is my end point for this goal? What do I need to do to get to that point?"* Suppose you've decided that you want to achieve an overall history test average of 90 percent. Right now your test average is 70 percent. To get to your end point, you will need to raise your average 20 percent. Maybe your end goal is to complete the obstacle course in gym class in under three minutes. Right now it takes you 4.5 minutes. You will need to improve your time by at least 1.5 minutes.

2. *List possible ways to get from your present point to your end point.* To accomplish the goal of a 90 percent average on history tests, your list might include taking better notes, listening better in class, beginning to study as soon as the test is announced, and studying with a friend. To improve your obstacle course performance,

your list might include improving sleep and nutrition habits so you feel more energetic, practicing the areas you have the most difficulty with, and practicing with a friend who can give you pointers to improve your performance.

3. *Organize your ideas into a plan.* List your ideas step by step in the order you plan to do them. Be specific about each step. Here is a sample plan for improving your history test grades.

- Listen in class.

- Take notes and review them each night.

- Read the textbook assignment and add important information to class notes.

- Once the test is announced, spend 45 minutes a night studying notes and memorizing details.

- Spend two hours on Saturday reviewing with a friend or having a parent quiz you.

A plan for improving your time on the obstacle course might look like this:

- Replace junk food with fruits and vegetables.

- Sleep eight hours a night.
- Spend 30 minutes a night on weak areas.
- Practice with a friend one night a week.
- Time self once a week and chart improvement.

4. *Talk to God about your goal regularly.* God wants to know how things are going. While He lived on earth, Jesus regularly talked with His Father. Right before He died, Jesus even asked God to confirm the way to accomplish our salvation. But Jesus didn't ask to get His own way; instead, He asked that His Father's will would be done. God sent an angel to strengthen Jesus for the walk to the cross. God promises to give you the same guidance and strength to achieve your goal or to change it.

5. *Do this for each of your goals.* Make your plan flexible. If you can't spend the full amount of time studying history because you have too much math homework, plan to study a little more the next night.

Check your
progress

Each week or month, check your progress. Ask yourself:

- Is my goal realistic?

- Is my game plan working?

- Am I closer to my goal today than when I started? than a month ago? than last week?

- Am I still interested in achieving this goal?

Check your progress for each goal and reevaluate your goal. Then rework your game plan to keep from giving up if you aren't progressing well or if you don't have the time or desire you first had for your goal. Reworking your plan doesn't mean you've failed. Reestablishing more workable goals will keep you from giving up in despair. And don't forget to celebrate when you achieve your goal.

So set some goals today and make a game plan. Find a friend to work with you to make it more fun. You'll be surprised at all you can accomplish as God keeps His promise to give you strength through Christ your Savior.

Now it's time for *you* to set some goals for yourself.

*Choose areas
for improvement*

Listed below are several areas in which you might want to improve. Put an X in the box beside each one that interests you, or add areas of your own.

❑ Advance academically

❑ Increase artistic ability

❑ Break bad habits

❑ Grow in Christian maturity

❑ Increase Christian service

❑ Improve fitness level/weight

❑ Expand musical ability

❑ Strengthen relationships with family (communicating, spending time with family, getting to know brothers and sisters better, etc.)

❑ Form/improve relationships with friends

❑ Improve relationships with teachers

❑ Enhance sports skills/learn new sport

☐ Increase study skills
☐ Participate in community service

*Choose one or
two focus areas*

Which areas for improvement are most important to you at this particular time? Go back and circle one or two areas from the list.

Set specific goals

Using the areas for improvement you chose, set one or two specific goals for each area. Write them below.

_____

_____

_____

_____

*Pray about
your goals*

Read John 8:12. How does trusting that Jesus is your leader (and the best goal-setter) affect the goals you set and how you achieve them?

_____

Read James 1:5. What does it say about wisdom?

_____

_____

Read Philippians 4:13. How does it apply to accomplishing your goals?

_____

_____

Write a prayer that asks God for His wisdom and strength to achieve your goals.

_____

_____

_____

_____

_____

*Make a
game plan*

Setting a goal is great, but you need to know how you will achieve it. For each goal you list, write down two or three steps you will take to achieve the goal.

Goal number 1 game plan:

A. ————————————————

B. ————————————————

C. ————————————————

Goal number 2 game plan:

A. ————————————————

B. ————————————————

C. ————————————————

Goal number 3 game plan:

A. ————————————————

B. ————————————————

C. ————————————————

*Check your
progress*

Begin with one or two goals now, then in a month, return to these pages. Reread your goals and review your game plan.

- Is your goal realistic?
- Do you still want to achieve it?

- Is your game plan working? If not, consider what needs to be altered.

- Are you closer to reaching your goal now than you were a month ago?

Revise your goals as needed each month. Once you've completed a goal, write another one to replace it. Aim high, pray about your goals, and with God's help, you can accomplish great things!

Verses for Thought

Trust in the LORD with all your heart and lean not on your own understanding; in all your ways acknowledge Him, and He will make your paths straight.

Proverbs 3:5–6

[Jesus] said, "I am the light of the world. Whoever follows Me will never walk in darkness, but will have the light of life."

John 8:12

2

Study Skills Guaranteed to Raise Your Grades

Does report card day leave you feeling disappointed and discouraged? Do your grades fail to meet your own and your parents' expectations? Developing good study skills will give your grades a boost.

Vince studied the grades on his report card, then stuffed it into his pocket. He considered throwing it in the trash, but his parents would find out sooner or later. He knew he was in for the "You're not working up to your potential" speech. It varied little from grading period to grading period.

Vince thought back over the grading period. It's not that he didn't try. He did. But even

*when he thought he was doing well, his grades
still fell short.*

Your Turn

Do your grades fall short of what you desire? Have you ever wondered if grades really matter? God probably doesn't look at the grade recorded on your report card, but He does care about the work you do!

It's important

Doing your best in school is important for several reasons.

- *God desires your best.* Ecclesiastes 9:10 says: "Whatever your hand finds to do, do it with all your might." God also tells us through the apostle Paul that "whatever you do, whether in word or deed, do it all in the name of the Lord Jesus, giving thanks to God the Father through Him" (Colossians 1:17). God wants us to use the gifts and talents He gives us to the best of our ability. When we do our best, we will be like lights on the hill, just as Jesus said (see Matthew 5:14–16).

- *The work habits you form now carry over into your adult life.* If you do just what you need to do to get by in school, you probably will do the same at your job later. If you form the habit of doing your best, that habit carries over into future jobs and makes you a valuable employee.

- *You will use what you are learning.* You may wonder why math or science or English is important, but you will use much of the knowledge you are learning. Whether you plan to be a businessperson, a church professional, a nurse, or even a truck driver, you'll need basic math skills to figure inventories and to handle money, basic grammar skills for talking to people, basic composition skills to fill out paperwork and make reports, etc.

- *Colleges will look at your grades.* Grades may not accurately reflect your progress in school, but college admissions personnel consider them. If you plan to go to college, polish up your grades now.

Grade killers

Poor grades occur for many reasons. Here are a few grade killers.

- Lack of preparation
- Inattentiveness in class
- Poor listening skills

- Poor note-taking skills
- Failure to do homework
- Failure to study for tests
- Poor test-taking skills
- Lack of background knowledge

Most of these can be overcome by improving your study skills.

Be prepared

You probably know students who arrive late to class without their textbooks, paper, pens, or homework. They aren't prepared! But having supplies and homework is only part of being prepared.

Review your notes nightly. Read ahead in your textbook. If you follow these simple steps, when you arrive at class the material will be fresh in your mind, you'll be ready to participate in class discussions, and you'll also have background information for the lecture.

Listen effectively

You spend a lot of time listening—more time than you spend reading, writing, or talking. You listen to your parents, teachers, pastors, and friends. Effective listening goes beyond just hearing the words. It requires skill and practice to concentrate on what's being said and to understand the words and their meaning.

- *Know why you're listening.* Are you listening for enjoyment, to understand instructions, to understand an assignment, or to learn new material? This makes a difference in how you listen. Listening to instructions means listening for step-by-step details. Learning new material requires listening to understand concepts. Know your purpose for listening.

- *Use the time lag.* The average person speaks at a rate of about 135 words per minute. The average listener can process almost 500 words per minute. Since you process information faster than your teacher speaks, it's easy to let your mind wander. Instead of thinking about lunch or what your weekend plans are, take advantage of the time difference to analyze the material and integrate it with previous knowledge. Formulate questions and organize the material in your mind.

- *Listen for concepts.* Sometimes people focus on details and miss major concepts. You may be so busy listening to the details of a war that you miss why the war occurred in the first place. Tie facts and concepts together, then recall other relevant information on the subject.

- *Don't tune out dry or difficult information.* It's hard to keep listening when you can't comprehend the material or when you just feel bored. Listen for things you do understand and for interesting pieces of information.

Listening involves more than hearing the words. It requires analyzing and organizing information in your mind.

Take notes

Most students make one of two mistakes when taking notes—writing down too much information or not writing down enough. Writing down too much information often means missing the overall picture or important details because of information overload. Not writing down enough means not having details that help to clarify the bigger picture.

- *Write down key words and phrases.* Don't try to record word for word what your teacher says. Use abbreviations whenever possible. Review your notes as soon as possible after class and spell out the abbreviations or fill in the gaps with information from your textbook or a friend's notes.

- *Follow along in your book.* If your teacher starts listing the reasons for the Civil War, jot down the page number in your textbook. Make notes of the information your teacher gives that is in addition to the material in the book.

- *Listen for tip-off phrases.* Comments like "The causes are …" or "The significance of the event was …" let you know the teacher is about to give important information that will help explain a concept.

- *Review your notes nightly.* Organize your notes and add information from the book. Read your notes aloud. This helps you remember the information longer and be more organized when it's time to study for the test.

*Complete all
assignments*

- *Make a page in your notebook to record homework assignments.* Divide the page into columns headed: *date, class, assign-*

ment, date due, done, and *grade.* Put a checkmark in the "done" column as you complete each assignment. Be sure to record the grade you received. This will help you monitor your progress.

- *Have a regular time and place for homework.* Stick to your schedule. Don't allow phone calls or television to interrupt your work. Organize your materials first so once you begin you won't waste study time looking for books, pens, or paper.

- *Start with the hardest assignment first.* Do the assignment you least want to do while you feel fresh. Work until it's completely done, then check it off your assignment list. Continue this way until all your assignments are done. Leave the easiest assignments for last when you least feel like doing homework. When you've completed all your assignments, take a break. Then check the assignments for mistakes and rewrite any that you need to.

Read effectively

You are required to do a lot of reading in junior high school. The amount of reading will only increase as you progress in school. Developing a plan of attack for reading makes your reading easier and more effective.

- *Preview first.* Whether you are required to read a whole book or just a chapter, preview it first. Look at the chapter titles or the headings of a chapter. Try to find the organizational pattern. Is the material arranged chronologically or by topic? Does it start by introducing a large topic and breaking it into sections, or does it start with small sections and work toward the whole? Look at pictures and read the captions. Notice any graphs or charts and their significance. Read the questions at the beginning or end of the chapter to help you know what to look for as you read.

- *Scan the written material.* Look for underlined or italicized words. Determine their importance. Find the definitions of any words you don't know. You also may want to scan the material specifically for answers to the questions given in the book or raised by your teacher during class.

- *Make questions out of headings.* Once you've completed the previous steps, begin reading the assignment a section at a time. Turn each heading into a question. "Causes for the Battle of Gettysburg" becomes "What were the causes for the Battle of Gettysburg?" If the title is "Natural Elements in Our World," ask yourself, "What are the natural elements in our world?" As you read, look for the answer to your question. Continue until you've completed the reading assignment.

- *Summarize.* List key points or major themes from your reading. Outline what you've read to help you organize information in your mind and remember it longer.

- *Analyze.* Go a step farther and analyze the material. Is it fact or the author's opinion? Does it agree with what you know and believe? Does it agree with what the teacher believes? How does it apply to you as a Christian?

*Start projects
early*

Avoid last-minute panic. Begin work immediately on research papers, book reports, science projects, and other long-term projects.

- *Choose your topic.* Go to the library the

same day you receive an assignment. Write down a list of possible topics and find out how many books or articles are available about each. Decide which topic suits you best.

- *Make a schedule.* Use a calendar to plan your project. Circle the project's due date, then work backward to plan your strategy. Suppose you have a month to write a paper about a great leader in America's history. Start from the date the paper is due and count back four days. Mark those days, "Prepare final copy." Count back another four days and mark those, "Have friend or parent proofread final draft." You've used eight of your 30 days. Count back another four days and mark those, "Edit final draft." Mark the six days before that "Revise and rewrite first draft." You have 12 days left to spend on research and writing your first draft. You can divide those days into separate times for research and writing your first draft or do both together. Stick to your time schedule to ensure you complete your paper the day it's due.

- *Set aside time daily.* Allow a certain

amount of time every night to work on your project to keep yourself on schedule. You may want to spend less time on weeknights and more on weekends. Plan according to what works best for you.

Ask questions and get extra help

If you don't understand some of the classroom material, ask questions. If you have trouble with an algebra equation, ask your teacher to demonstrate more problems. Keep asking until you do understand. If you find yourself leaving class each day wondering what your teacher was talking about, arrange for a tutor or for extra help from the teacher after school. Don't hesitate to get the answers you need.

Follow Through

How do your study skills measure up? Ask God for wisdom and help in making needed improvements, confident that He will do what is best for you.

Be prepared

Are you prepared to face class each day? Check all the phrases that describe your normal class preparations.

- ☐ Homework done and ready to turn in.
- ☐ Class notes reviewed from the previous day.
- ☐ Reading completed and future reading scanned for the main ideas.
- ☐ Supplies and textbooks placed in a location where they won't be forgotten.

Strengthen any areas you couldn't check.

Listen effectively

Effective listening takes practice. On the left are positive listening skills. On the right are poor listening skills. Rate yourself.

__ Know why you're listening	__ Listen because you have to
__ Use time lag to integrate information in your mind	__ Use time lag to decide where to go on your next date or what to wear to school the next day

__ Listen for concepts and details

__ Listen just for details you might have to memorize

__ Listen even if the information doesn't interest you

__ Daydream away those dull lectures

Did you rate more as a positive listener or a poor listener? Apply your listening skills to church, time with friends, and family time too. What steps will you take to become a more positive listener?

Take notes

Keep these key ideas in mind:

- Write down key words and phrases.
- Listen for tip-off phrases.
- Copy your notes nightly.
- Borrow notes from someone who has good notes, comparing them with yours to see what you've missed.

*Do all
assignments*

Make a page in your notebook like this:

Date	Class	Assignment	Date Due	Done	Gra

List all assignments. If you have overdue assignments, see if the teacher will accept them late for partial credit. If not, do them for your sake. Skipping even one assignment may mean missing important information.

Read effectively

Do you have a lot of reading to catch up on? Keep these important steps in mind:

- Preview first.
- Scan the written material.
- Make questions out of headings.
- Summarize.
- Analyze.

Start projects early

It's easy to procrastinate on projects—especially if the assignment is one you don't particularly like. Unfortunately that makes it harder for you in the long run. Why not start projects today? Do you have a book report due? Visit the library and select a book. Do you have a science project to do? Look at library books containing projects or surf the Internet for ideas. List several projects that interest you. Read through the projects and decide which one would be best for you. Do you have a research paper to write? Choose your topic today!

Find a calendar and circle the due date of the project or report. Now count backward and mark off days to do each step of the project—make a neat final copy, edit and revise your final draft, write your final draft, edit and revise your rough draft, write your rough draft, and research.

Ask questions and
get extra help

Are you having trouble with a certain subject or with schoolwork in general? Here are some things you can do.

- Talk to your guidance counselor.
- Ask your teacher for extra help after school.
- Talk to your parents about getting a tutor.
- Arrange to study with another student or friend.

Don't ignore problems. They probably won't go away—they'll get worse!

Verses for Thought

Wisdom is supreme; therefore get wisdom. Though it cost all you have, get understanding.

Proverbs 4:7

And this is my prayer: that your love may abound more and more in knowledge and depth of insight, so that you may be able to discern what is best and may be pure and blameless until the day of Christ, filled with the fruit of righteousness that comes through Jesus Christ—to the glory and praise of God.

Philippians 1:9–11

3
Taking the Test

Have you ever studied for a test only to fail it? Do you get a nervous stomach or sweaty palms when it's test time? Test anxiety affects many students. Learning to overcome it will improve your test scores.

Alex looked at the test lying facedown on her desk. She knew she'd failed without even picking it up and looking.

"What'd you get?" her friend Brandon whispered from behind her.

Alex raised the corner of the test and looked. Then she held it so Brandon could see it.

"Fifty-two percent! What happened? You knew all the material when we studied Saturday!" Brandon exclaimed.

"I don't know," Alex said. "I just forgot everything when Mr. Smith handed out the test.

My test scores are killing my grades."

Your Turn

Do you ever feel like Alex? There's hope. Through the apostle Paul, God tells us, "Do not be anxious about anything, but in everything, by prayer and petition, with thanksgiving, present your requests to God" (Philippians 4:6). He has promised to help you when you call on Him—even if the problem is test anxiety or raising your grades. Even if you don't suffer from this problem, the following material will help you better prepare for tests. First, let's look at tests in general.

Do tests matter?

Some educators feel schools should not give tests. They feel that tests don't really show whether students know the material or not. Some students, like Alex, know the material but do poorly on tests. They panic or just don't take tests well. Other students who don't know the material can fake their way through tests and receive good grades. Educators who don't believe in tests feel it would be better to grade students on class performance and how well they can apply what they've learned.

Whether or not these educators are right, tests probably will be around for a while, so it's best to master test-taking.

Preparing starts many weeks ahead of the test date. As soon as the teacher introduces a new unit or new material, your work begins.

Get organized

- *Block out an uninterrupted study period each night.* Make a list of what you need to study. Then break that list into manageable tasks.

- *Become disciplined in your approach to study.* Don't lose the first 10 or 15 minutes trying to find books, papers, etc. Have everything at your fingertips so you can maintain your focus on the material.

- *Budget your study time.* Tackle the hardest work first while you're fresh. Decide how long each assignment should take and try to complete it within that amount of time. If you find your mind wandering, set a timer to remind yourself that your allotted amount of time is dwindling.

- *Review the study skills in the last chapter and apply them to your study time.*

Get help early

- Ask for help as soon you start having trouble. Don't wait until just before the test to get help. That doesn't leave you enough time to study and prepare.

- Study with a friend who does understand the information. Quiz each other on the information.

Know what to expect

Knowing whether the test will ask essay, short-answer, or multiple-choice questions, as well as knowing what chapters it will cover, helps you study more effectively.

- For short-answer or essay tests, have a good grasp of the concepts covered in the chapter. Have an overview of the material in your mind and an idea of significant events, people, theories, and concepts, as well as how they relate to one another.

- For multiple choice or true/false tests, pay additional attention to detail, such as dates, names, places, equations, titles, authors, etc.

Relax the night before the test

- If you've been studying each night and following the suggestions in the chapter on study skills, just review briefly the night before the test. After your review spend the evening doing something relaxing and fun.

- If you have trouble sleeping the night before a test, do something physical— run, bike, shoot baskets, or play racquetball—to use up your nervous energy.

Start the test day out right

- Try to sleep eight hours the night before a major test. You'll need a clear mind, and a good night's sleep is essential for removing the cobwebs.

- Eat a good breakfast. Too much sugar can hinder clear thinking. Eat a high protein breakfast for energy.

- Ask God for wisdom and calmness.

- Get to class a couple of minutes early so you're not in a rush.

Relax as you go into the test. Breathe deeply and let tension drop away. Pray for guidance as your teacher passes out the test. Once the test starts, listen to the instructions and read the directions for yourself. Know exactly what the question is asking before you attempt to answer.

- *For an essay question:* Read the question and decide what information is needed to answer it completely. Are you writing about a person's life or just one accomplishment? Are you summarizing a story or analyzing it? Jot down your thoughts. Arrange them in a logical sequence before you begin to write. Include only what is needed to answer the question.

- *For a short-answer question:* Follow the same steps as the essay question but make sure your answer is brief and concise.

- *For a multiple choice or true/false question:* For either type of question, only one answer is right, and the others are wrong. There's no in-between. For a multiple-choice question, read the question first and have the answer in your mind before you read the choices. See if one choice matches the answer you've thought of. If not, eliminate obvious wrong answers, then choose the best remaining answer. For a true/false question, read the statement. Make sure you read it correctly. If you aren't sure of the answer, try reversing the question and see how it sounds to you.

- *For a matching section:* Read both columns of the matching section first. Then read down the left side. Have an answer in mind before searching the right side for a match. Do the pairs you know first, then do your best to make logical matches for the others.

- *For an open-book test:* Study the material as thoroughly as you would for any other test. Write your test answers from memory, then use the book to check your answers and fill in what you don't remember. You won't have time to search the book for information and also have time to formulate well-written answers. Be familiar with the chapter organization so you can quickly find the additional information you need.

Make sure you have answered all the questions. It's better to guess and have a chance at getting some points than to not try at all. Blank spaces won't get you any credit.

Reread the test. Did you mark the answer you intended? Did you answer each question thoroughly? Is your writing legible?

Overcoming test-day nerves

Everyone reacts differently to tests. Some students have a mild case of the butterflies. A few students become so nervous they can't function normally. Those with a severe problem should seek the help of their guidance counselor or teacher.

One way to help calm test-day nerves is to be so thoroughly prepared that you don't have to worry about anything. You can face the test, confident that you're ready.

If you start to panic, stop for a minute. Relax and breathe slowly. Give yourself a mental pep talk. Remind yourself that you know the material and will do well on the test. Be confident that God is with you, helping you to remember what you've learned and calming your fears.

Keep a Bible verse in mind, such as

Hebrews 13:5, "Never will I leave you; never will I forsake you," or Philippians 4:13, "I can do everything through [Christ] who gives me strength." These promises of God are true—even when applied to schoolwork or tests. Your heavenly Father, who cared enough to send Jesus to rescue you from your sins, also cares enough to help you through an exam.

If your mind goes blank, don't panic! Reread the question. Look for key words. Try to think of anything associated with that subject. Write down anything that comes to mind. Try to visualize your teacher talking about the subject. Or visualize your notes. Let your mind digest these things, then reread the question and attempt to answer it. If you still can't come up with the answer, move on. Perhaps a later question will help jog your memory. Don't forget to come back to any unanswered questions. Always make an attempt to answer the question, even if it's only a guess.

Review test performance

After the test, review your performance and think of ways to improve your study or test approach. When you get your test back, notice weak areas to improve before the next test.

Test day doesn't have to signal failure. Prepare well, approach the test confidently, and ask God to help you do your best!

Follow Through

Use the chart on the next page and the suggestions given in the chapter to plan your study time and your approach to taking the test.

Fill out the chart as completely as possible for all upcoming tests.

Verses for Thought

> But seek first His kingdom and His righteousness, and all these things will be given to you as well.
>
> *Matthew 6:33*

> He who began a good work in you will carry it on to completion until the day of Christ Jesus.
>
> *Philippians 1:6*

Date	Class	Chapters/Material included	Date of test	Type of test

4
Making Time

Do you have trouble finding time for all you need to do? Do you frantically complete homework and projects the night before they are due or look for your books, sheet music, and sports uniform as the bus pulls up? This chapter will help you decide what deserves your time as you create a workable schedule.

Mallory looked at the clock. It couldn't be 10 P.M. already! She still had math homework to do, a history test to study for, an outfit to iron for the next day, and her room to straighten up.

"Are you almost finished?" her mom called. "You should be in bed."

Mallory slammed down her pencil in frustration. Why was there always so much to do and no time to do it? She never seemed to have time for fun. Homework and her part-time job took every spare moment.

Your Turn

Time can't be recycled. It's never regained. To make the most of your time, plan! By organizing, you will get more done *and* have more time for yourself. Learning to manage minutes now will save you stress and extra work in the future.

List overdue
projects

Note the work you haven't yet completed. List

- Overdue homework assignments
- Neglected household responsibilities
- Upcoming projects and papers
- Half-finished leisure projects

Be thorough and list even small items, such as letters you owe friends and relatives. Then arrange these items in order of priority. Put the most important item at the top of the list.

Start with item 1 and work until it is completed. Proceed to item 2. When you've assembled your list and begun to mark off completed projects, it's time to develop a time-management program for the future.

Make a list of everything that demands your time and how much time each activity takes each week. This will help you see what demands your attention. You may be surprised at how much you are trying to fit into one week, not to mention one 24-hour period!

Include these items:

- Church _____
- Youth group activities _____
- Music lesson(s) _____
- Homework _____
- Club meetings _____
- Part-time job or baby-sitting _____
- Responsibilities at home _____
- Sports (practices and games) _____
- Hobbies _____
- Special times with friends _____
- Other _____
- Other _____

*Make a written
schedule*

By putting an hourly schedule on paper, you will see how many hours a day you have to work with. Write the days of the week across the top of the paper and the hours down the side.

- *Pray about your top priority.* God can help you decide what most deserves your time. But remember to give God top priority. Consider how important Jesus thought it was to spend time with God. Your heavenly Father knows the many demands placed on you. He wants what's best for you, and He's already working to accomplish it.

- *Schedule absolutes first.* Consider church, your quiet time with God, part-time job, and other essential activities that meet at a certain time each day or week.

- *Plan around extracurricular activities, clubs, sports events, and other inflexible schedules.*

- *Schedule activities that need to be done but not necessarily at the same time each day.* These may include piano practice, homework, and household jobs.

- *Use the remaining time for activities you wish to do, such as time with friends, television, or reading.*

Keep up-to-date

Schedule a little time each day, for assignments, projects, and household jobs. Don't wait until the weekend to clean your room or study for Monday's test. You will avoid Sunday night panic and additional stress.

Start early

Start long projects early. Choose a topic for your science fair project or term paper as soon as it is assigned. Begin gathering materials to avoid rushing or staying up late the night before the project is due. You can relax as you work on your project because you know you have a good start and plenty of time to complete it.

Organize

You will save time if you take time at the beginning of each work session to gather and organize your materials. Locate books, pens, and notes first. Once you're organized, begin work and complete the tasks at hand.

Plan leisure time

Your schoolwork and other responsibilities are important, but include quality activities for enjoyment too. Plan a long bike ride with a friend or a workout on the racquetball court to help you think clearly. Trying to go full speed without a break leads to burnout, and you won't have the desire or energy to do your best.

Put these timesaving steps into practice today, and you will be surprised how much you can accomplish!

Follow Through

Time to get organized! Have you put off projects? Have you neglected a task? Is homework long overdue? List any of these overdue items in order of priority with the highest at the top.

— 1. _____
— 2. _____
— 3. _____
— 4. _____
— 5. _____

Start with item 1 and work at it until it's completed. Check it off the list and move to the next item. Continue until you've completed the list.

Make a schedule

- Schedule your quiet time with God.
- Block out times you are at school and church.
- Write in the hours you are at your part-time job or when you baby-sit.
- Note sports practices and games, clubs, and other activities that meet at a certain time daily or weekly.
- Budget time for your household responsibilities, homework, long-term projects, and other obligations.

	Sunday	Monday	Tuesday	Wednesday	Thursday	Friday	Saturday
A.M.							
P.M.							

- Each week, schedule at least two periods of two hours each for leisure time. Plan to make the most of it!

Stick to the schedule for a month, then revise it as needed. Update your schedule as priorities and time demands change.

Verses for Thought

There is a time for everything, and a season for every activity under heaven.

Ecclesiastes 3:1

My times are in Your hands.

Psalm 31:15a

5

Facing a New School

A new school means making new friends and adjusting to new teachers, a new building, and a whole new life. You may face entering a new school because you've moved to a new neighborhood or because of the transition from elementary school to junior high or from junior high to high school. This chapter will give you tips for adjusting.

Lauren fumbled with her locker combination, willing it to open. She'd lost her way trying to find her locker after math and only had two minutes to get to her next class. Yanking the locker door open, she searched the school map for her next classroom, then leaned against her locker in despair.

A sea of unfamiliar faces swarmed by, but no one stopped to ask Lauren if she needed help. Tears welled in her eyes. Her last school had only 20 classrooms situated along two hallways. This building seemed to have 200 rooms and endless hallways. She had known everyone at her old school and considered most of them friends.

"If only I were back at Lincoln," she whispered. "I'll never make friends here—I'll never even learn my way around this school!"

Your Turn

Attending a new school is difficult for most students. Whether you move from an elementary school to a junior high or move across the country to a new city and school, it means change.

Most of you have faced or will face a move to a new school. If some of your same friends are making the move with you, it may not be as difficult. You will have someone to share the anxious moments with, and you don't have to deal with a new house and neighborhood at the same time. Whatever the reason for attending a new school, preparing ahead can help.

*Gather
information*

If you learn you are moving to a new city because a parent gets a new job or a transfer, write for information about the city and surrounding areas. You can write to the chamber of commerce in that city to request information. If you are in a military family, ask to see brochures about the new base.

Write to the local school system. Inform them of your new address and find out what school you will attend. Request a map of the campus. Familiarize yourself with the map, as well as the school's location in the neighborhood.

Know what to expect from your new city.

- Is the area urban or rural?
- Is the city large or small?
- How many schools are there?
- What attractions are nearby?
- What is the weather like year-round?
- How many malls are there? bowling alleys? skating rinks?
- What sports teams play in the city? Don't forget to ask about amateur and college teams too.

Find out all you can about your new school.

- What classes are offered?
- How much choice do you have in selecting classes?
- What clubs are offered?
- What social activities does the school have?
- What committees can you serve on?
- What sports are offered?
- Is there a school newspaper? a yearbook?

- Are there musical or dramatic groups that perform?

If you are entering junior high school in the same school district in which you attended elementary school, you may be given a tour of the school along with an information packet. If not, request both. Ask about orientation for incoming students.

Find a contact
person

If you're moving from elementary school to junior high, you may have older brothers or sisters who attended the school or still attend it. If so, arrange to go to school with them the first day. If you don't have older brothers or sisters, search the neighborhood for someone who attends the school.

If you've moved to a new city, you may not have met many kids yet. Look around your church for students near your own age. Some of them may attend the same school you will attend. Call the school and ask if there are student volunteers who help new students find their way. Many schools have this type of program or would be willing to pair you up with a partner for the first day.

Visit the school

If possible, visit the school before your first day and take a tour of the facility. If you know what classes you will be taking, find out the room numbers. Jot down notes and plan your route as you walk through the building. Locate your locker and practice the combination.

Seek out a friend

Seek out another new student or someone you recognize from your neighborhood or church youth group. Look for someone who's eating alone in the cafeteria or library, and approach that person. Take a risk. You may make a lifelong friend!

Follow Through

Are you facing a new school? Find out the answers to these questions:

- How many students attend the school?

  _____

- What are the school colors?

  _____

- What is the team name? _____

- What is the mascot? _____

- Is there a newspaper and/or a year-book? _____
- Is there a band, orchestra, and/or choir? _____
- Were any plays or musicals performed last year?

  _____

- What elective classes are offered?

  _____

  _____

- What clubs are available? _____

  _____

- What sports are offered? _____

  _____

Look at the class and activities list. Write down which classes, clubs, activities, and sports interest you. Consider trying something new.

1. _____

2. _____

3. _____

4. _____

5. _____

Arrange for a tour of the school. Find out the answers to these questions:

- Where is your locker located? _____
- What is the room number of your homeroom? _____
- Where is the cafeteria? _____
- Where is the gym? _____
- Where is the library? _____

List the room number of your classroom for each period if you know them.

Period	Course name	Room number
First	_____	_____
Second	_____	_____
Third	_____	_____
Fourth	_____	_____
Fifth	_____	_____
Sixth	_____	_____

Verses for Thought

The LORD Himself goes before you and will be with you; He will never leave you nor forsake you. Do not be afraid; do not be discouraged.

Deuteronomy 31:8

And surely I am with you always, to the very end of the age.

Matthew 28:20

6

Making Friends

Do you have one or more close friends? Do you meet people easily? Whether you've just started at a new school or could just use another close friend or two, this chapter will give you ideas for forming new friendships.

Robin slouched at the lunch table, her food tray untouched, as she watched groups of students talking and laughing all around her. "I wish I were part of one of those groups," Robin whispered. "I wonder how it would feel not to eat lunch alone every day."

Robin isn't unfriendly, just quiet—and that makes it hard for her to make friends. She spends most of her time alone.

Robin stabbed at the peas on her plate. "If I could find one other lonely person I'd have a friend," she said out loud. But everyone around her looked happy and content. It was going to be a long school year, Robin decided.

Your Turn

Making friends is easy for some people and hard for others. Which group do you fall into? Whether you make friends easily or the thought petrifies you, some basic steps will help.

*Know what you're
looking for*

Friends have a big influence on you, so it's important to consider what kind you want. What are you looking for? What is most important to you—a sense of humor? good looks? strong values? loyalty? faith in God?

A real friend is one who shares the good times, as well as the bad. Real friends care about and help each other. David and Jonathan are perhaps the most well-known Bible friends. The Bible describes their friendship as, "Jonathan became one in spirit with David, and he loved him as himself" (1 Samuel 18:1). Jesus, your Best Friend, loved you so much that He gave His life for you on the cross. And because He rose again, you will be with Him in heaven forever. Jesus said, "Greater love has no one than this, that he lay down his life for his friends" (John 15:13). While you may not have to sacrifice your life like Jesus did, true friends care about others. Don't settle for less!

Make a list of your own beliefs, standards, and interests. How will these affect your friendships? For instance, you may want a friend who goes to your church or one who shares your love of reading. Or maybe truthfulness and dependability are more important to you. Deciding what you want in a friendship ahead of time will help you know when you've found a good friend.

Go where there
are kids your age

Sitting at home alone won't help you make friends. Be in contact with other kids—the kind you want to get to know. Check out these places to find peers who share your values and interests:

- Church youth group
- City youth rallies
- School Bible studies
- Special interest clubs
- Sports teams or events
- Newspaper or yearbook staff
- Tutoring programs

- Choir or band
- Church or city service programs
- Volunteer organizations

*Be friendly
to everyone*

If you set your sights only on making friends with the in-crowd, you may set yourself up for disappointment or be tempted to compromise values and beliefs. Be friendly to everyone and ask God to bring you the friend you need. It may be the quiet math whiz, the person who sits behind you in science class, or someone you meet at the library. Be open to different personalities and individuals, but be true to your Christian beliefs.

Make the
first move

Don't wait for others to notice you. If you are in a big school, you may never be noticed! Say hello to those sitting near you in each of your classes. Find out people's names and use them in your conversations. Ask about their other classes, their church, or their family. Try to find common interests. You soon will have an idea of which classmates would be interesting to know better. Invite one or two classmates to your house to do homework or to study for a test together. Ask them to a youth group party or activity. Let people know you are interested in being friends.

Be a good listener

Encourage others to talk about themselves, then really listen. This will give you clues to hobbies, interests, problems, and values. Listen to the meaning as well as to the words. You may learn more from a tone of voice and from body language than by what's actually said. Listen for the underlying emotions, fears, or joy.

Remember what your friends like to talk about and ask more about those topics later. This will let them know you listen and care.

Be dependable

Do what you say you will do, when you say you will do it. If you plan to meet at the mall at 7 P.M., be there at 7 P.M. People need friends they can count on. If you get into the habit of not showing up or calling when you say you will, you'll soon have a reputation for being unreliable.

Your friends also need to be able to depend on you to stick with them in difficult times. Fair-weather friends aren't really friends at all.

Be courteous

No one wants to be with someone who is rude or who ignores the basics of appropriate behavior. Your everyday manners say a lot about you. Interrupting, being loud, and dominating conversations turn people away quickly. Think of others and let their interests and needs be as important as your own.

Be upbeat and positive

It's hard not to be friends with someone who is genuine, warm, and enthusiastic. This isn't to say that you can't share the tough times you are facing with your friends, but few people want to be friends with someone who is constantly complaining or blue. Learn to be joyful inside, and it will show on the outside.

Take your time

Don't try to rush friendships—they take time to develop. Trying to get too close too fast makes you appear pushy or clingy. Watch for clues as to how fast the other person wants the friendship to develop too.

Accept rejection

Not everyone will like you. Don't let this hurt you or keep you from trying again. Popularity doesn't reflect on your self-worth. Some personalities just don't fit well together. Use times of rejection to evaluate your life and improve yourself if needed. Then go on and try again.

Losing friends

Making friends is only half the battle. Keeping them requires effort on your part too. The following friendship killers can quickly cost you friends.

- Neglecting your friend when someone better comes along.
- Borrowing clothes and social standing.

- Being negative, whining, and complaining.

- Dominating conversations with stories about yourself.

- Being envious of your friends' money, talents, boy/girlfriend, etc.

- Gossiping about your friends.

- Being critical of your friends and your friends' other friends.

- Unloading your problems on your friends but being too busy to listen to their problems.

- Being possessive and displaying jealousy when your friends spend time with other friends.

- Trying to top everything your friends do.

Making and losing friends is part of life. Even Jesus experienced rejection by His closest friends (remember the Garden of Gethsemane?). Ask God to help you avoid the friendship killers and instead keep your focus on building and maintaining strong friendships. With His help, you can make and keep good friends during your school years.

As you experience the ups and downs of friendship, remember that the number of friends you have or whether you're part of the "right" group is unimportant. What's truly important is knowing your Best Friend is Jesus. He always stands by you. His death and resurrection have won you forgiveness for the times you fail your friends. And when your friends let you down, Jesus is ready to comfort you with the knowledge that He loves you unconditionally and always will.

Follow Through

Do you want to make new friends? Ask God to help you be the friend you should be and to bring the right friends to you.

What beliefs, values, and interests do you want your friends to share? List them in order with the most important at the top.

1. _____
2. _____
3. _____
4. _____
5. _____

Where can you go to meet those who share your values and interests? List some ideas below.

1. _____
2. _____
3. _____
4. _____

5. _____

What strengths do you have to offer a friendship—loyalty, a listening ear, a sense of humor? List the traits you hope others will see in you.

1. _____
2. _____
3. _____
4. _____
5. _____

Look around you this week. Are there potential friends? Introduce yourself. Listen as you talk with these people and take steps toward cultivating friendships.

Verses for Thought

A man of many companions may come to ruin, but there is a friend who sticks closer than a brother.

Proverbs 18:24

Very rarely will anyone die for a righteous man, though for a good man someone might possibly dare to die. But God demonstrates His own love for us in this: While we were still sinners, Christ died for us.

Romans 5:7–8

7
Sharing Christ with Friends

Are you a Christian attending a public school? Do you want to share your faith with peers but don't know how? This chapter provides practical tips on sharing and living your faith in the classroom.

Kareem paused on the front steps of Washington Junior High School. It was his first day as a student here, and he wasn't sure what to expect. Would there be other Christians? Would he have a chance to share his faith—or courage if he did have a chance? Would the classroom discussions conflict with his beliefs?

"God, help me face whatever is ahead," Kareem prayed. "Give me the courage to hold onto my faith and share it with others."

He pulled the door open and entered, feel-

ing like Daniel on the way to the lions' den.

Your Turn

Sharing your faith doesn't have to be frightening. Instead, it can be a natural part of your life. You can show others that being a Christian is a joyful and fulfilling way to live!

*Your training
program*

No successful athlete competes without training and preparation. Witnessing requires training and thought too. As the Holy Spirit works in your life through the Scriptures, He will make your Christian witness effective. As Jesus tells us, when the time comes to tell others about our Savior, "the Holy Spirit will teach you at that time what you should say" (Luke 12:12).

- *Have a daily quiet time.* Spend time reading God's Word. Choose to read a devotional book written for teens or a chapter of the Bible each morning. Be consistent. Spend time in prayer. List special requests, including the names of those with whom you want to share your faith. Ask God to prepare their hearts.

- *Be regular in church attendance.* Attending Sunday school, church services, and youth activities builds you up and helps you to grow as the Holy Spirit works through God's Word. You will constantly learn new things about the Christian life and how God is at work in you through His Word, which is alive in you.

- *Fellowship with other Christians.* Form close friendships with peers who can encourage and join you in talking about your faith.

*Sharing your faith
one on one*

You don't have to be a missionary or pastor to share your faith. You just need the desire. These suggestions will help you get started.

- *Ask God to help you live a consistent Christian life.* Your friends watch your actions. Displaying a bad attitude, swearing, cheating, or goofing around in class hinders your message.

- *Invite friends to youth activities.* Friends that won't attend church may attend a youth rally or a pizza party. Be specific in your invitation. Instead of asking,

"Do you want to go to youth group with me some time?" ask, "Would you like to come to our youth group game night Friday night? I can pick you up at 7 P.M." People will respond quicker to a specific invitation.

- *Ask God to make you ready to share your faith.* Be prepared if someone questions why you attend church or why you don't participate in certain activities. Use this as an opening to share your faith in Christ.

- *Memorize Bible verses that show God's plan of salvation.* Find Scripture passages that present the basic plan of salvation. You probably know John 3:16, but try these passages too:

1. Everyone has sinned—Romans 3:10, 23

2. Sin separates us from God—Romans 5:12; 6:23

3. Christ, the perfect Son of God, died for our sins and was raised from the dead—Romans 6:4; 6:23

4. Everyone who believes in Jesus as their Savior will have eternal life—Romans 6:23; 10:9

Use these verses to explain God's plan of salvation. As you read your Bible or participate in Bible studies, highlight and memorize other appropriate passages.

Living your faith
in the classroom

Sometimes you'll have the chance to share your faith in the classroom. This doesn't mean standing on your chair and waving your Bible in the air. It does mean being consistent with your faith and being prepared to give clear answers about what you believe.

- *Avoid confrontations.* If a teacher makes a comment that conflicts with your beliefs, think before replying. Would this be the best time to say something? If so, what is the best way to convey your message?

- *Have a positive attitude.* Arguing, getting mad, condemning others, or displaying a bad attitude about schoolwork won't help you portray victorious Christian living. Ask God to help you remain positive, mature, and in control.

- *Don't refuse to answer questions or do homework.* If a test question conflicts with your beliefs, don't refuse to answer it. You might say, "The textbook states that ..." or "According to the class lecture ..." If you receive a homework assignment that involves reading or watching something inappropriate for a Christian, talk to the teacher about an alternative assignment. If you get no results, talk to your parents about the situation.

- *Involve your Christian faith in your schoolwork whenever possible.* Here are some ideas:

  Write a history report on the Reformation, the persecution of the early church, or another event from church history. Or focus on the part Christianity played in the life of a person, such as George Washington, Christopher Columbus, or Joan of Arc.

  Write a book report for English on the biography of a great man or woman of faith, such as Augustine, Mother Teresa, Martin Luther, or John Bunyan. Or choose a novel by a Christian author and encourage others to read it.

  Choose a science project that points to God's hand in nature or the laws of science. Make the presentation outstanding!

These ideas will make sharing Christ with

friends in your classroom a natural way of life for you.

Follow Through

Are you ready to share your faith? Let's get started!

- *Prepare a faith statement.* Write a brief paragraph about your faith in God and what it means to be a Christian. Avoid lingo others wouldn't understand such as "saved" or "sacrament." Include what Christ has done for you and what He gives to all people who trust in Him as their Savior.

_____

_____

_____

_____

_____

_____

- *Memorize Bible verses that explain God's rescue through Christ.* Choose those listed in this chapter or pick others. Write the verses on the next page.

87

Everyone has sinned.

_____

_____

_____

_____

Sin separates us from God.

_____

_____

_____

_____

Christ, the perfect Son of God, died for our sins and was raised from the dead.

_____

_____

_____

_____

Everyone who trusts in Jesus as their Savior will have eternal life.

_____

_____

_____

_____

- *Look for ways to share your faith in the classroom and through your schoolwork.* What current assignments could allow you to share your faith?

_____

_____

_____

_____

Verse for Thought

In your hearts set apart Christ as Lord. Always be prepared to give an answer to everyone who asks you to give the reason for the hope that you have. Do this with gentleness and respect.

1 Peter 3:15

8

Patching Up Friendships

Do you feel distant from a friend? Have you lost a friend because of a misunderstanding or conflict? This chapter analyzes the reasons friendships dissolve and how to repair them.

Cyndy and Trina, once best friends, barely speak to each other as they pass in the school hallway. A five-year friendship ended abruptly at the beginning of the school year.

Cyndy, who had a secret crush on Jon, confided her feelings to Trina. When Jon asked Trina, not Cyndy, for a date and Trina accepted, Cyndy felt betrayed and refused to talk to Trina. Jon and Trina are no longer dating, and Cyndy and Trina remain detached. Neither Cyndy nor Trina feels it is her responsibility to mend the friendship.

Your Turn

All friendships have rough times that threaten to end the friendship. King David wrote about one friendship gone bad in Psalm 55. David says he could handle it if his enemies had insulted him, but it's a friend who has turned against him (Psalm 55:12–14). Or think about how Jesus felt when Peter denied Him by the fire.

But Jesus was no ordinary friend. He had come to earth to win forgiveness for sinners—even for Peter, His close friend who had betrayed Him. Jesus' death and resurrection removed the damage of sin forever so we could be part of God's family.

Just as God didn't give up when Adam and Eve sinned but set into motion His rescue plan, don't give up on a good friendship. It's worth it! Ask God to help you do what it takes to reconnect with your friend.

*Evaluate your
friendship*

Consider the reasons your friendship first formed. Were you on a sports team together or assigned to the same group for a project? Are you neighbors or in the same church youth group? Do you share common interests?

How do you feel now? Do you enjoy spending time together? Are your interests still similar? Considering these things helps you decide if a friendship is worth saving.

When friends
grow apart

Friends may drift apart over time. A close grade-school friendship dwindles in junior high. Or your closest junior high buddy seems distant in high school. There are many reasons for this.

- You develop different interests.
- You make new friends.
- You are in conflict over values.
- You mature at different rates.
- You have separate schedules or schools.

It is natural to form new friendships over time. This differs from friendships that end abruptly because of a fight or misunderstanding.

Fractured
friendships

Misunderstandings, betrayal of trust, and disagreements can end friendships. When one of these threatens a relationship, determine whether you should work to resolve the problem and restore the friendship or just let go. Is the problem solvable and the relationship worth saving? Most relationships can be mended.

Mending fractured friendships

Determine to take steps toward restoration whether or not the conflict was your fault.

- *Analyze the conflict.* What went wrong? What underlying feelings, motives, or disagreements played a part? Could it have been handled in another manner with different results?

- *Talk it out.* Arrange a time for the two of you to be alone. State your feelings in a positive way. Avoid criticism or cutdowns. Ask God for wisdom in choosing your words. You may say something like, "I know we are having a problem right now, but I hope we can work it out. Our friendship means too much to me to end it over this situation." This starts the conversation out in a positive manner. Continue to use "I statements" to explain your views and feelings rather than accusatory "You statements."

- *Listen with an open mind.* Hear your friend out. You may be viewing the situation from two different perspectives. When you thought your friend was ignoring you at the party, he may have been trying to reach out to a new peer. Or when you felt your friend was being clingy, she may have been displaying her insecurity. Listen to your friend's words and the feeling behind them. Ask questions to clarify the situation.

- *Accept blame.* Swallow your pride and admit any wrongdoing. Be honest about your feelings, conduct, and motives. Ask your heavenly Father— who sent His only Son to win your forgiveness on the cross—to strengthen you to forgive your friend whether or not the friend accepts blame or apologizes. Holding a grudge wears you down.

- *Leave it behind.* If you are able to restore the friendship, leave the hurts behind. Don't bring them up later.

- *Let go.* Despite all you do, your friendship may end. If differences are too great to reconcile or values too different, let go gracefully. You still have memories of shared times. Treasure these and pray for your friend. Use what you've learned from this friendship to build a new, stronger friendship with someone else. What you've learned through difficulties may make you a better friend later.

Most friendships have a few bumps and bruises along the way. When times are rough, Jesus, your heavenly Friend, is by your side. He gives you the power to follow His example of forgiveness and friendship. He will help you overcome any problems and strengthen the relationship.

Follow Through

Evaluate your friendships. Have they suffered from misunderstandings, hurt, feelings of betrayal, or even unkind words?

- *Set a time to talk.* Stop and call your friend now.

- *Evaluate the problem.* When did the problem start? What caused it? How can you best convey your feelings to your friend?

- *How could the situation have been handled differently?* What could you have done?

- *List ways to keep the problem from recurring and ways to strengthen your relationship.*

_____

_____

_____

_____

- *Evaluate the friendship.* What strengths do each of you bring to the friendship?

You	Friend
_____	_____
_____	_____
_____	_____
_____	_____

What areas do you need to strengthen?

_____

_____

_____

Verse for Thought

Do nothing out of selfish ambition or vain conceit, but in humility consider others better than yourselves. Each of you should look not only to your own interests, but also to the interests of others. Your attitude should be the same as that of Christ Jesus.

Philippians 2:3–5

DECIDE FOR YOURSELF

9
Choose the Best

Do you face decisions about participation in certain activities? Is it hard to discern what a Christian should and should not do? This chapter presents principles to guide you in making the best choices.

Maurice studied the poster on the school bulletin board. Everyone was talking about the big concert Friday night. Patrick walked up and read the poster. "Wow. A free concert here at school. I'm not going to miss this! You're coming aren't you?" he asked.

"I don't know. This group is known for doing some pretty wild things. Some of their music is okay, I guess. I'll have to think about it," Maurice said.

Maurice sat at the kitchen table that night. "I really don't think I should go," he said to his brother. "But everyone else is going—even the Christian kids. I don't want to be left out or have people think I'm 'different.' Why are these decisions always so hard?" he asked.

Your Turn

Are you facing some tough decisions? As a person entering adulthood, you must make choices. You decide what to wear to school, what to eat for breakfast, what classes to take at school, what clubs to join, what sports to play, what committees to serve on, and much more. While the Bible doesn't give us a specific list of right and wrong activities for today's teen, it does give us principles to help us make good choices. Four principles are found in 1 Corinthians.

Choose activities that are beneficial

" 'Everything is permissible for me'—but not everything is beneficial" (1 Corinthians 6:12a). Sometimes an activity, though not bad in itself, serves no real purpose. Watching television or going to movies, cruising around in a car, hanging out at a fast-food restaurant, and other activities aren't wrong, but why not choose ones that challenge you or build you up mentally, physically, or spiritually? Church activities, family times, and some school events meet this standard. Try one of these:

- Learn a new sport, such as racquetball or volleyball.
- Take up an aerobic exercise, such as biking or inline skating.
- Learn to cook.
- Play a game, such as chess, to challenge your mind.
- Try a game, such as Outburst or Scattergories, for family fun.
- Learn a new hobby, such as photography or sewing, that could lead to a future job.
- Take a lifesaving or water safety class.
- Join math or Spanish club.
- Write or take pictures for your school paper or yearbook.
- Take part in a church ministry.
- Start a new Bible study.
- Join a youth choir.
- Learn to play a musical instrument.

*Choose activities
that won't
control you*

" 'Everything is permissible for me'—but I will not be mastered by anything" (1 Corinthians 6:12b). Some activities start out as harmless recreation but end up as addictions. An example is sports. We become involved in sports for fun and recreation, but it soon dominates our thoughts. Nothing matters more than succeeding in or watching that sport. It is constantly on our mind and begins ruling our lives. The same thing can happen in other areas, including:

- Watching television
- Listening to music
- Playing video games
- Participating in a club or hobby
- Studying

While the activity in itself isn't bad, if it masters your time, money, or thoughts, it's time to look for a change of activities. Jesus occupies first place in our lives as our Lord and Savior. We need to get rid of anything that threatens to replace Him in our lives.

*Choose activities
that strengthen
you physically*

Jesus' death and resurrection redeemed not only your soul, but your body too. Consider what God tells us through the apostle Paul: "Do you not know that your body is a temple of the Holy Spirit, who is in you, whom you have received from God? You are not your own; you were bought at a price. Therefore honor God with your body" (1 Corinthians 6:19–20). Some things are obviously harmful to your body, such as getting a tattoo, smoking, drinking, or taking drugs. But most of us are guilty of staying up too late, eating too much, or neglecting to exercise. Too much exercise also can have a negative effect on your body. Keep your body in maximum physical shape by:

- Getting at least seven hours of sleep a night.
- Eating three well-balanced meals each day.
- Choosing healthy snacks, such as fruit, vegetables, or lowfat yogurt.
- Drinking lots of water, especially in hot weather or when exercising.
- Participating in an aerobic sport, such

as biking, running, or inline skating for at least a half hour three times a week.

*Choose activities
that glorify God*

"So whether you eat or drink or whatever you do, do it all for the glory of God" (1 Corinthians 10:31). Do others know you are a Christian by your actions? Christians are responsible for bringing honor to God's name. If you are participating in activities that weaken your Christian walk or Christian witness, it's time for a change. Choose activities that point others to Christ or show them a more abundant lifestyle. Not all of your activities need to be spiritual in nature, but they should be above reproach. Read Ephesians 4:20–5:2. List ways that Ephesians says God will help you "imitate" Him in your activities and show the love of Christ to others.

Ask God to help you use these four principles to choose activities that are beneficial and not addictive, activities that build you up physically and are pleasing to Him.

Follow Through

List your favorite activities below. Include

sports, hobbies, clubs, church activities, and social times.

1. _____
2. _____
3. _____
4. _____
5. _____
6. _____
7. _____
8. _____
9. _____
10. _____

Reread each item you listed. Decide if they are physically, mentally, emotionally, or spiritually beneficial. Put a *P, M, E,* or *S* after each one to indicate in what area it benefits you. Some items may be beneficial in more than one area and some in no area. Reconsider the items that have no benefit. Are there other activities you could replace them with?

Of the items you listed, do any of them master you? Do they control your time, thoughts, or money? Put a *T* after any activity that dominates your time, a *TH* for thoughts, and an *M* for money. Rethink these activities. How can you change their hold on your life? Is it time to replace them with new activities?

Are at least some of the activities ones that will build you up physically? Do any of them harm your body? Circle any that have a negative effect on you physically. Decide how to change or replace those activities.

Of the activities listed, which ones portray victorious living in Christ? Search God's Word to find activities that will please Him and provide a Christian witness.

You have many activities to choose from. Consider the principles given and choose only the best activities.

Verse for Thought

"I have come that they may have life, and have it to the full."

John 10:10b

10

Positive Peer Pressure

Are you faced with negative peer pressure? Do you wish it were easier to do what is right? From the very beginning, Christians have been concerned with these questions. This chapter will show you how to exert peer pressure of your own.

Trent slowed down as he walked out of school. "Looks like they're at it again," he said to his friend Logan. They watched as a group of six guys lit up cigarettes and piled into two cars. "I get so tired of guys like that. They smoke on school property and everyone thinks they're so cool!" Trent exclaimed.

"Yeah, it seems like the 'bad' kids get all the attention. I guess going to Sunday school, singing in church choir, and studying hard to

get good grades isn't thought of as cool," Logan said. "I wish we could win kids over to our side as easily as the crowds that are into smoking, sex, and stuff like that."

Your Turn

Do you feel like you're the only one trying to live God's way? Does it seem that smoking, sex, and hanging around with "the wrong crowd" is the cool thing to do? Sometimes it is hard to stand up against negative peer pressure. But not only can you stand up against it, with God's help you can exert some positive peer pressure! Think about what God has to say to you through the words of Peter: "Since Christ suffered in His body, arm yourselves also with the same attitude ... [do] not live the rest of [your] earthly life for evil human desires, but rather for the will of God" (1 Peter 4:1–2).

Realize the power
of peer influence

Everyone is influenced by friends. It's not wrong to wear popular clothing or shoes as long as the styles are modest and are acceptable for a Christian. It's natural to want to fit in with the group, and that's fine too, as long as the members of the group share your Christian values and beliefs.

Seek friends who are a positive influence

Friends play an important role in our lives. They influence how we act, talk, dress, what activities we participate in, and even what television shows we watch. Choose friends who will build you up, encourage you to make good choices, and stand with you when the going is tough. Look for others who are involved in wholesome activities and will support you in the same.

Stand up for right

There are many students who are against smoking, premarital sex, swearing, cheating, and other negative practices. But they may be too timid to admit to their values. Be the first to stand up and say no to wrong actions. You don't have to campaign in the school hallways, just look for opportunities to put in a positive word. When a conversation turns to sex, stand up for your beliefs. Say, "It may sound old-fashioned, but I am waiting for marriage. It is a gift my spouse deserves. Besides, with the spread of AIDS and other diseases, it's the practical thing to do." You may lose a few friends, but you'll gain some who feel the same way you do.

Seek out positive groups and clubs

Get involved in organizations such as teen groups against alcohol, drugs, or abortion, or participate in Christian organizations and clubs. Investigate programs such as peer tutoring or counseling. Be a part of organizations where you can make a difference and can have a positive influence in the life of another student, your school, or your community.

Find alternatives

Don't settle for just avoiding the negative, look for positive alternatives. There are many fun and exciting activities Christians can participate in. Chapter 11 will look at creating activities for yourself and others.

Follow Through

How do others influence you? Consider your clothing, television viewing, leisure reading, activities, and even the way you talk.

In what areas do others most influence you?

_____

_____

_____

_____

Is the influence a positive or negative force in your life?

Do you have friends who will support you in exerting a positive influence in your school? Are there other students who share your ideals? List people you think would help exert positive peer pressure.

_____

_____

_____

_____

Talk to these students and share some of your ideas and goals. If they are interested, schedule a time to meet together to plan and pray.

Check the community page of your local paper or ask at your school office about organizations that are making a difference. Find out as much as you can about each. Choose ones that allow you to make a positive impact. List your ideas on the next page.

_____

_____

_____

_____

Verse for Thought

Don't let anyone look down on you because you are young, but set an example
for the believers in speech, in life, in love,
in faith, and in purity.

1 Timothy 4:12

11

Creating Your Own Activities

Are you tired of missing social events because they aren't appropriate for Christians? Do you wish for more acceptable activities to choose from? This chapter will help you create activities for yourself and your friends.

~

"Hey, Rachel, did you hear about the big party Drew's having next Friday?" Kendal asked his friend.

"Who hasn't heard about it?" Rachel replied.

"Guess it's going to be the party of the year," Kendal said.

"Yeah, free beer and R-rated videos. Sorry, I'm not interested." Rachel said.

"I'm not either, really, but I get tired of

missing out on everything," Kendal said.

"Well, that's one party I'm not sorry to miss," Rachel said. "He's going to be in real trouble if his parents come home early. But I know what you mean about missing out. It seems like everything has to do with drinking or sex or the occult. It's hard to find things to do. I wish we had more teens at church so we could do things together as a youth group," Rachel said.

"So what are we going to do Friday night while everyone else is at Drew's party?" Kendal asked.

"Stay home as usual. Maybe I'll start my science project," Rachel said with a shrug.

Your Turn

Is your social life suffering because activities include drinking, forbidden movies, unchaperoned parties, or other inappropriate things? You don't have to sit at home. Create your own activities!

*Enlist the help
of friends*

Talk to friends and students in your classes. Check out their feelings about social activities. Look for friends at church who are in agreement with you. Hold a planning meeting. Invite everyone over for pizza. Have pen and paper ready to make some plans.

List alternatives

List negative social activities that have taken place recently. Or perhaps there have been no social activities and you want to plan some. List positive alternatives to each. For instance, your school is planning a Halloween party that centers around the occult, fortune-telling, and so on. Plan your own activity. Have an all-night video marathon with everyone bringing favorite movies and snacks to share. If your school is planning a big dance featuring one of the worst rock bands you've ever heard, plan a date night with your friends. Dress up and use the money you would have spent on the dance to go to a nice restaurant.

Spread the word

Invite others to join you. Let them know you aren't trying to compete with the other event, just offering an alternative. You will form new friendships and increase your social life.

Talk to school officials

If school activities are repetitious, maybe it's time for a change. Suggest new activities for your school. Offer to help plan a harvest festival instead of a Halloween party or a banquet instead of the usual dance. Be creative and invite others to help. You may be surprised at how many students are ready for a change.

Plan church-related activities

Talk with your youth leader about inappropriate school events. He or she may not realize the problem. Discuss the possibility of your youth group having one big social event a month.

Try something new each month. Have a pizza party and movie one month, go bowling or skating the next, and have a gym night another month. Plan creative activities, too, such as a "Stuff Night." Divide into teams. See which team can stuff the most people into a phone booth, compact car, bathtub, and so on.

Plan a progressive dinner. Meet at one person's house for appetizers. Then travel to another house for salad and on to another for the main meal and another for dessert.

Don't feel left out. Plan creative, fun activities for you and your friends.

Follow Through

List social activities that you've had to miss because they were inappropriate for Christians.

_____

_____

_____

_____

List possible alternatives.

_____

_____

_____

List friends who would help you plan alternative activities.

_____   _____

_____   _____

_____   _____

List ideas to present to your school officials or youth leader. Consider ideas for Halloween, Christmas, banquets, sports events, graduation trips, parties, etc.

_____

_____

_____

_____

Verse for Thought

Let your light shine before men, that they may see your good deeds and praise your Father in heaven.

Matthew 5:16

12
Don't Give Up

Do you ever feel like giving up? Do you dream of walking out the school doors and never returning? This chapter will look at those feelings and help you make plans for the future. If you are doing well in school, this chapter will allow you to think about the future and what God has planned for you.

"I've had it with school," Jonathan said. "I'll never use all this junk we're learning. I wish I could just quit!"

"Yeah, but then what would you do?" Sarah asked.

"I don't know. My dad quit school and joined the Navy at 17, but now you have to have a high school diploma to join the service. What a bummer!" Jonathan said.

"Yeah, but you only have three and a half years to go. That's not so long," Sarah said.

"Three and a half years if I pass all my classes. I'm getting Ds in math and science and an F in English. The only things I'm doing well at are gym, shop, and art. I get so tired of the same lecture every grading period, 'You can do better. Your brother Mark made straight As and got a scholarship to college.' I hear it every time I take a report card home," Jonathan said. *"I just want to get out of here, forget school, and get some kind of job!"*

"What kind of job?" Sarah asked. *"You want to work at a fast-food restaurant all your life?"*

"No, but anything has to be better than school! What am I going to do?" Jonathan asked in despair.

Your Turn

Have you ever wondered if school was really worth it? Do you have trouble earning top, or even passing, grades? Is it difficult to meet the expectations held by your parents or teachers? Many kids feel this way. Some drop out of school either by not paying attention or by leaving at the first opportunity. Others struggle on until they finally graduate. Still other students overcome the obstacles and finish well. Which group do you fall into?

The dropouts

Around a half million teens drop out of school each year. Some of them are right in your own town. There are many reasons why teens drop out of school. Here are a few.

- Poor grades
- Failure
- Lack of friends
- Lack of support from parents
- Lack of proper clothes and supplies
- Desire for employment and money
- Need for employment to support family
- Drug and alcohol use
- Pregnancy
- Boredom
- Older than classmates
- Parents or siblings were dropouts

Once they've made the decision to drop out, few teens return to school. They are older than other students in the same grade. Friends and classmates already have graduated or would graduate ahead of them.

Seek help

Even a bad situation can be turned around. Meet with your guidance counselor to discuss ideas. You may receive a tutor or a chance for extra after school help. This may not be your idea of a good time, but it could make the difference.

Look at the classes you're taking. Are they too hard? Are you being asked to perform on a college preparation level when you really want to take general classes? Talk with your guidance counselor and parents about needed changes.

Some cities offer a vocational education program or a career center. You take core classes at your high school in the morning, and in the afternoon you focus on your selected career, such as small machine repair, secretarial skills, and so on. Perhaps this program would be helpful to you. Consider these alternatives as you move ahead in your school career.

Consider
your options

Once you've completed high school, you have many options. Many students go to college, but it isn't for everyone. If you didn't enjoy high school, studying, or sitting in classes, you probably wouldn't care for four more years of it. College has advantages over high school, such as being able to choose what classes to take and how many to take at a time. You may want to enroll for a semester and take a variety of classes to see if it's for you.

Some students go to technical school to learn a career such as electrical wiring, secretarial skills, mechanics, or appliance repair. Look for the technical school closest to you and see what it offers.

Military service is always an option. You can enlist for four years and learn job skills while receiving an income, living facilities, and food. After basic training you will have some choice as to where you are stationed. If your first enlistment goes well, you can opt to make the military a career.

Stay in school and look to the future. It holds promise for you. God has a plan for you. Turn to God's Word for direction in your decisions.

Follow Through

Are you having problems at school? What things bother you most? List them.

_____

_____

_____

_____

What can you do to solve each problem? Talk to your parents or guidance counselor for ideas.

_____

_____

_____

_____

What do you plan to be doing a year from now? five years from now? ten years from now? Write down some ideas.

_____

_____

_____

_____

Ask your guidance counselor, parents, or youth leader to help you find information about colleges, technical schools, military service, or other areas of interest. Study the information and pray about what God wants you to do.

From the beginning, God has known you. He planned for your salvation before you were even born. Jesus came to earth to win you forgiveness and eternal life through His death and resurrection. Your God, who loves you enough to sacrifice His only Son, also loves you enough to give you everything you need for this life. You can trust in His wonderful plan for your life.

Verse for Thought

"For I know the plans I have for you," declares the LORD, "plans to prosper you and not to harm you, plans to give you hope and a future."

Jeremiah 29:11

Discussion Questions

Chapter 1

1. What are some reasons that resolutions and goals often fail?
2. Have you had resolutions you've quickly forgotten about?
3. How do you know God cares about your goals?
4. What are some steps to setting goals you can achieve?
5. What is the importance of making a game plan?
6. How does checking your progress on goals keep you on track?

Chapter 2

1. Why is doing your best more important than the grades you receive?
2. Do you feel grades are important or that there is a better way to chart progress?
3. Why is it important to develop good work habits now?
4. How does being prepared help you do better in class?
5. How is "listening" different from just hearing the words?
6. What are some steps to getting more out of what you read?

Chapter 3

1. What is test anxiety?
2. How can it keep you from doing well on tests?

3. Have you ever done poorly on a test because of nerves?

4. How did you feel about it?

5. What are some ways to overcome test-day nerves?

6. What Bible verses can you remember to help you?

Chapter 4

1. What does "Time can never be recycled" mean to you?

2. Why is it important to have a plan for your time?

3. Do you find that you don't have enough time to do all you need to do?

4. What things fill up most of your time?

5. What things should have first priority on your time schedule?

6. Why is leisure time important?

Chapter 5

1. How did the transition from elementary school to junior high affect you?

2. Did you have friends or siblings to help you?

3. What things helped you adjust?

4. Why is preparation for the transition important?

5. What thing would be most important to find out about your new school?

6. What is the most important part of school for you?

Chapter 6

1. What do you look for in a friend—common interests, good personality, faith, etc.?

2. What qualities are most important to you in a friend—honesty, loyalty, etc.?

3. What strengths can you offer a friendship—humor, loyalty, etc.?

4. What things draw you closer to your friends?

5. Did you ever have a time when it was hard to make friends? How did you overcome it (or how will you overcome it)?

6. What things cause you to lose friends?

Chapter 7

1. What is the most difficult part of being a Christian in a public school?

2. How can having other Christian friends help?

3. What ways of sharing your faith are easiest for you?

4. What is hardest?

5. What ways of sharing your faith in your classroom have you found successful?

6. Which have not worked?

Chapter 8

1. How does losing a friend because of conflict differ from growing apart?

2. What things cause friends to grow apart?

3. Have you ever experienced this?

4. What things can end friendships?

5. What steps can you take to mend a friendship?

6. What should you do if it can't be mended?

Chapter 9

1. How do you decide what activities to be a part of?

2. What biblical principles can help you decide?

3. Have you ever had to leave or quit an activity because it wasn't appropriate?

4. What are some ways that activities can benefit you?

5. How do some activities control you?

6. What can you do if you feel an activity is beginning to control you?

Chapter 10

1. What is peer pressure?
2. Is peer pressure always bad?
3. When is peer pressure good?
4. How do friends influence you?
5. Does this mean you always must have Christian friends?
6. How can you exert positive peer pressure?

Chapter 11

1. What activities has your school had that you couldn't take part in?
2. How did you feel about being left out?
3. Do you know of others who were left out?
4. Does this mean Christians can't have a full social life?
5. How can you plan alternative activities?
6. What are some activities you could plan?

Chapter 12

1. What are common reasons students drop out of school?
2. Why do they seldom return?
3. What are some alternatives to dropping out?
4. Why is staying in school important for securing a job?
5. What are some of the different options for high school graduates (college, the military, etc.)?
6. How can a student know which option is right for him or her?